# Dancing to America

*Dancing*

# to America

Ann Morris   *photographs by* Paul Kolnik

DUTTON CHILDREN'S BOOKS    NEW YORK

*This book would not have been possible without the kind help and gracious cooperation of the School of American Ballet, its administration, teachers, children, and the spirit behind their work.*

Text copyright © 1994 by Ann Morris
Photographs copyright © 1994 by Paul Kolnik
(with the exception of the photographs on pages 8–9, 10, and 12)
*Coppélia* photograph on page 15 © Choreography by George Balanchine
and Alexandra Danilova after Marius Petipa

CIP Data is available.

Published in the United States 1994
by Dutton Children's Books, a division of Penguin Books USA Inc.
375 Hudson Street, New York, New York 10014

Designed by Amy Berniker

Printed in Hong Kong   First Edition   ISBN 0-525-45128-5
1 3 5 7 9 10 8 6 4 2

This is the story of a young Russian ballet dancer, Anton Pankevich, and his family, and their search for freedom and opportunity in the United States. It is a search that many people who came before them have made.

In the years before Anton and his family came to the United States, the Soviet Union, as the country was then called, was governed by the Communist party. Under Communist rule, it was difficult, if not impossible, for people to express themselves in an open manner. Even if they wanted to, they were not free to leave the country. The government persecuted people who had ideas or religious beliefs that differed from the official ones. The Pankeviches' decision to emigrate to America was made in the hope that they would find a different, freer life for themselves and their children.

After Anton's family left the Soviet Union, there was considerable turmoil and many changes took place there. Republics broke away from the strong centralized government and set up separate, independent states. It was, and still is, a time of uncertainty and difficulty for the Russian people. The city in which the Pankeviches had lived, Leningrad, which was named after the founder of the Communist party, Vladimir Lenin, became known again as St. Petersburg, its name before the Communists came to power in 1917. There is no longer a single country called the Soviet Union; but despite the movement away from a strong central state toward greater democracy, there is still some religious persecution, as well as limits to artistic expression.

ANTON PANKEVICH loves to dance. Ever since he was a young boy, his dreams and hopes and efforts have converged on one goal: to become a famous ballet dancer like his idols, Mikhail Baryshnikov, Rudolf Nureyev, and Natalia Makarova. These three great dancers had first been stars in Russia, Anton's birthplace. Four years ago, Anton left Russia. Now he is sixteen and a student at the School of American Ballet (SAB) in New York City. It has been a long journey.

Anton was born in Leningrad, the city most closely connected to the Russian ballet tradition. He was taught the foundations of ballet in a school that reflects this powerful tradition, which has influenced the style and the performance of dance all over the world. It was passed on to Anton directly by his father, who had also trained to be a ballet dancer.

Growing up in a ballet family, Anton had a strong sense from early childhood of what he wanted to do with his life. He was selected to attend the elite Vaganova Academy, where many of Russia's most famous dancers had learned their art. Ballet school there was not luxurious, but it had an air of elegance that was a reminder of the time when it was the Imperial Ballet School, belonging to the czar's ballet company, which put on performances at the famous Maryinsky Theatre. His teachers there were strict, but they inspired his love for the art.

At the Vaganova Academy, which was named after a famous teacher and former director of the school, Anton attended both ballet and academic classes. They were housed in a historic building on one of Leningrad's most beautiful streets—"Theatre Street," as it is known. Anton lived at home, which was quite near the school, whereas other young dancers, who came from all over the country, had to live in dormitories at the school.

The classes were demanding, and the children were expected to behave in a way that would instill in them the necessary discipline and determination to master this exacting and physically tiring way of life. Anton and his classmates felt privileged to be learning these traditions that had been handed down from the great Russian teachers and choreographers. There were opportunities to learn from teachers who had danced the great ballet roles and who had taught famous dancers.

The children in the school worked long and hard hours. They were expected to put considerable effort into both their ballet and academic classes. But the rewards were many. Everyone in Russia looked to these students and felt pride in their contribution to this most beloved of Russian arts. Dance recitals, Christmas parties, performances, and the thrill of participating in such a noble endeavor were all part of Anton's early experience.

TOP: *Anton's class at the Vaganova Academy*    ABOVE: *Anton in* Paquita, *Kirov Ballet*

*Rudolf Nureyev (left) with Anton and his father at Lincoln Center, New York City*

*Natalia Makarova with Anton and admirers in Washington, D.C.*

But dancers in Russia had little chance to explore developments in ballet in the West. The names of Anton's idols—Nureyev, Baryshnikov, and Makarova—were rarely mentioned in Russia, because they had fled the country (which is called defecting) and settled in the United States. Although Baryshnikov is one of the world's most famous dancers, his picture did not hang on the walls of the Vaganova Academy with the others who had studied there before going on to become great dancers. Anton would meet Makarova and Nureyev later in the United States. Russia was a difficult country for artists, who need freedom of expression as well as opportunities to see what is happening in other parts of the world and to exchange ideas with people in their profession.

In addition to the artistic restrictions, Anton's family had difficulties with the KGB, Russia's secret police, partly because Anton's grandmother was Jewish. After much thought the Pankeviches decided to come to the United States. Friends told them that there would be more freedom to choose what you want to do, to say what you think, and to worship whomever and however you please. They also heard from dancers who had left that they would have more freedom to work. Anton was then twelve. When he told his classmates that he was going to America they didn't believe him.

The Pankeviches planned their departure carefully. There were so many things to think about: what they would take, where they would stay, how they would earn their living. During the months of preparation, Anton thought back to the many wonderful times he'd spent with his friends and family at their dacha, a cottage in the countryside near the historic city of Novgorod. He remembered the bears he'd seen in the woods and how his father had rescued him once when he'd fallen through the ice on one of the freezing winter days.

The family packed all the things they thought they would need in their new life, including their precious samovar for serving tea, photographs, and ballet programs that would recall their life in Russia.

The law imposed limits on the amount of money they were permitted to take out of the country, so Anton's father, Victor, bought three expensive tins of black caviar, which he thought he would be able to sell for much-needed dollars. However, the Russian customs officers who examined all their belongings before they boarded the airplane took the caviar away from them. This angered and worried them, and also reminded them that Russia was not a country where they wished to live. Finally, Anton and his father left for the United States. Anton's mother and his seven-year-old brother, Sasha, followed seven months later, once Anton and Victor had found a place to live.

When he first arrived in America, Anton traveled around the country, dancing and taking classes in several cities. His first stop was a visit to Russian friends in Pennsylvania—the same friends who had invited them to the United States. Anton remembers how new everything was to him—the language, the food, school, the landscape, even the animals. "The first one I saw was a deer," he recalls. He had only seen deer before in books or on television. He also remembers how he marveled at his first movie, *Star Wars*. He sat through it several times. He and his father traveled on to Iowa, where other friends welcomed him to their dance studio, and then went on to Canada, Washington, D.C., Chicago, San Francisco, and finally, New York—where everything awaited Anton.

New York is the dance capital of the United States, and the home of the finest ballet companies in the country. It is the city where the great choreographer George Balanchine, who had also attended the czar's famous ballet school, had finally settled after he left Russia. Balanchine's name is well known to *everyone* in the ballet world—even in Russia. So of course the Pankeviches had heard of him. Balanchine, too, had wanted to expand his knowledge of the world and of ballet and to have more opportunities to create dances in a new style. He had come via Europe to the United States, and there he started the New York City Ballet (NYCB) and the School of American Ballet, which trained the dancers for his company.

Anton auditioned with Antonia Tumkovsky, one of the several Russian teachers at the school. She has had many years of experience teaching young dancers and recognized Anton's talent and spirit. He was immediately admitted to Balanchine's School of American Ballet at Lincoln Center.

Victor and Anton's first home of their own in New York was a small apartment in Brooklyn, not far from Brighton Beach. This area has a large community of recently settled Russians. They felt particularly at home in this neighborhood with its Russian shops, newspapers, and the sound of Russian voices. At first, they didn't have any furniture, so they slept on the floor. After continually searching the streets of their neighborhood, they were able to find a bed and a few chairs that someone had thrown away. They pulled an old washing machine up five flights of stairs to their apartment.

Anton and his father found all sorts of jobs to do: Victor delivered apples; Anton packed boxes in the supermarket; and on weekends the two of them walked alongside the railroad tracks and collected empty cans for recycling. Because they had had to leave so many things behind in Russia, they wanted to earn as much money as they could in order to build a new life. Slowly, they made their small home more cozy.

Anton loved his new city. He took the subway into Manhattan—for classes, rehearsals, and performances. The trip to the ballet school took over an hour, which was very different from when he had lived so near the Vaganova Academy in Leningrad.

Anton tried to attend as many performances of the New York City Ballet as he could. The first ballet he saw in New York was *Coppélia*. Anton was impressed! He noticed the precision and the musicality of the performance, and how the dancers' movements seemed to be much quicker than what he was used to. Would he ever be able to become that kind of dancer, he wondered. He wanted to know all about this new style of ballet. This way of dancing certainly was different from the Russian style, and he had to understand exactly why and how.

*NYCB production of* Coppélia

As he explored his environment, he found it filled with the distractions and riches of life in New York. He learned how to navigate his new surroundings by himself. "Things are always open in this city," he said. "I like it so much."

But it was not all easy. Frequently he was tired from the journey back and forth from Brooklyn to Manhattan in addition to a full day of classes and rehearsals. One night he was beaten up on the subway by a gang of boys. The ways of the West were different. There were fewer rules, and some that he did not understand. There were so many decisions and choices to be made. Anton had always been mischievous. He liked to play tricks, to fool around, to "do his own thing." He was high-

spirited and enjoyed playing boyish pranks. Sometimes this was misunderstood. It took time for Anton to learn the ways of American teenagers.

He also had to learn what his ballet teachers expected of him. Though less strict than at Vaganova, they had their own standards of behavior. Classes at SAB were different from those at Vaganova, too. Everything moved just a little bit faster. Anton was not always certain what the teachers were telling him or showing him. He had spent many years learning the classic steps and movements of Russian ballet. They were part of his heritage and of the vocabulary of dancers in the country where he was born. Now ballet steps had to be relearned according

to the principles of George Balanchine, who had made his own modifications of the classical technique and execution when he came to America. But Anton was eager to learn as much as possible, to be exposed to many styles and approaches, and to do well in his new country.

Many of his teachers at SAB had been born in Russia or other European countries and either spoke his language or were familiar with the style in which he had been trained. They too had had to adjust to their new country, to Balanchine's technique and this new style of dancing when they first came to the United States. This was reassuring to Anton and gave him confidence.

Additionally, the pressure to excel was al-ways upon him. Anton was aware that his family depended on him. They had sacrificed a life that was familiar and given up security and friends so that he and his brother would have opportunities that were impossible to obtain in Russia. They wanted him to succeed—to become a star in the ballet world. All this was a heavy burden for a young boy about to become a teenager, a boy who needed to find his way in a new country so different from the one he had left, who needed to be his own person distinct from his parents, who had left one culture and become part of another.

Since their arrival in New York City the Pan-keviches have lived in three different apartments. Now their home is near the ballet school, which means more time for sleep and less time on the subway. Time is very important to Anton, because he is so busy with ballet class, rehearsals, and auditions. He also has his academic studies at the Professional Children's School, a special school for children in the performing arts. Anton says it is much easier than his school in Leningrad. History is the subject that interests him the most. He has lived some of his history and geography lessons in his travels between countries and cultures. He has already mastered English and speaks some French, the language of ballet. Anton would like to spend a couple of years in Paris, which also has a long ballet tradition, when he finishes his formal education. Anton jokes about the skeleton in the science lab, saying, "Even though you have to be thin to be a dancer, you don't have to be *that* thin!" He has made new friends, and they help each other. Anton likes to be with his new friends at the Professional Children's School and at SAB, but he also needs to spend time studying at home by himself.

It is exciting to be living in a new country, but it is difficult, too. The family brought from Russia all of their pictures and old programs from the Kirov Ballet, along with photos and videos of their favorite dancers. They look at these pictures often to remind themselves of all they left behind. "That's when I danced in *Paquita,*" recalls Anton. Elena, his mother, serves tea throughout the day. "An old Russian custom," says Anton. "We used to make it in our samovar." In New York they are more apt to make their tea from tea bags.

Victor, Anton's father, works as a physical therapist in a doctor's office in New York. Elena works in a supermarket near their house. She worked in a market in Leningrad, too, but things were different. Sometimes there was no food for sale. And even when there was, the people would have to wait in long lines to buy whatever was available.

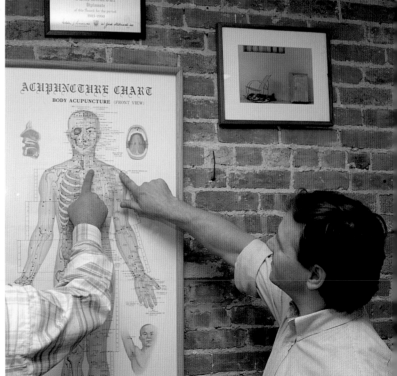

Classes at the School of American Ballet take up most of Anton's time. He practices at the barre, performing the positions and movements that are required in order to strengthen his muscles and prepare him for the many different dance steps. In one of his classes, he learns by imitating the gestures of his teacher, Stanley Williams. Anton has to practice the same movements over and over again until his muscles have learned them. Sometimes members of the company join the classes. Darci Kistler, one of the principal dancers with the New York City Ballet, studied with Stanley when she was a student at the school and sometimes still takes class there.

Many students grow very fond of their teachers. The teachers, in turn, are proud of their dancers and sometimes keep in close contact with them throughout their careers. Anton enjoys watching Darci and the various members of the company. When he is alone he practices things he sees them do. He knows that whether his teachers are watching him or not, he has to keep on working and learning and finding his own way.

Adam Lüders, formerly of the Royal Danish Ballet and now a principal dancer with the New York City Ballet, is another of his teachers. When Adam teaches he helps everyone, often by demonstrating. His suggestions extend from head to toe and might include anything from how to point a foot to how to keep his hair out of his eyes. Here Anton gets special help from Adam. He pays careful attention to what he says, and after class he continues to practice what he has learned.

Anton knows that a dancer must take risks. He has fallen many times, but he gets up and goes on to the next jump or turn. As the great dancer Fred Astaire once sang, "I pick myself up, dust myself off, and start all over again."

In adagio class Anton learns how to dance with girls. This is called partnering. After finishing a combination together, he and his partner, Tara, smile. With another girl, Jenny, he performs "the fish," a step that is supposed to resemble the way a fish looks. Male dancers have to do special exercises to strengthen the upper part of their body so that they will be strong enough to hold and lift their partner.

Anton has a special rapport with one of the
Russian teachers, Andrei Kramarevsky, who is
fondly called "Krammy." Krammy, a former
dancer with the Bolshoi Ballet, speaks with Anton in Russian about his dancing. In class they
are now concentrating on jumps. Anton men-
tally goes through his steps. At Vaganova he
was instructed to take more time to prepare for
these steps. At SAB he learns Balanchine's
method, which stresses preparation as part of
the movement. This is one of the things that
Anton has to work on repeatedly.

Anton jokes with another Russian member of
the school, the accompanist, Alla Edwards. Like
most young people, he enjoys fooling around,
sometimes to the exasperation of his teachers.
Ballet is mostly serious business, but humor and
playfulness are also important aspects of creativ-
ity. And it's so hard to be serious all the time!

Accompanists have special musical skill.
Alla's job is to play the tempo and rhythm re-
quested by the teacher and to improvise on famous ballet themes. The dancers follow the
music with their movements. All dancers must
acquire some knowledge of music as part of
their training. They must be able to dance to
the rhythms exactly and to feel the mood the
music is trying to convey.

Ballet has always stressed continuity and tradition. The great ballerina Alexandra Danilova shares her memories and mementos from her days of dancing with Balanchine and the Ballets Russes. Anton, his brother, Sasha, Susie Pilarre (a teacher at SAB and a former dancer with NYCB), and her two daughters, Zoe and Halley, both at SAB, listen carefully as Madame Danilova tells them about her life in ballet. She talks with Anton and Sasha in Russian, asking them where they lived in Russia and what they are working on now. Such experiences are a special treat for Anton and recall happy memories of his home in Russia.

Madame Danilova, who taught at SAB for many years, still comes to the school on special occasions to share her knowledge and experience with students. She always conveys some of the distinctive qualities of passion, wit, and elegance that made her a great and innovative ballerina who flourished in Russia, Paris, and other centers of ballet in the first half of the twentieth century.

SAB is fortunate to be part of Lincoln Center, the cultural heart of New York City and the home of the New York City Ballet, the Metropolitan Opera, and other art groups. World-famous companies of dancers and singers give performances there while on tour. When the Kirov Ballet came to New York to dance at the Metropolitan Opera House, Anton was happy to see two dancers there from his home in Leningrad, Konstantin Zaklinsky and Altynai Asylmuratova, who dance with the company.

Anton is proud to have been chosen as one of the principal dancers in a production at the Metropolitan Opera, Benjamin Britten's *Death in Venice*. He auditioned with many other boys and is particularly pleased to have been selected for a leading part. All his hours of effort are beginning to bring him closer to his goal of becoming a professional dancer.

But Anton is certainly not an all-work-and-no-play person. He has many friends and has especially enjoyed spending time with them in Central Park, in the middle of Manhattan. Anton, his friend José, Sasha, and Sasha's friend Eric enjoy themselves in Strawberry Fields, the part of Central Park that is dedicated to John Lennon, one of the Beatles. At Bethesda Fountain, the boys try to fish their Frisbee out of the fountain. But if they're not careful, Anton could be the next thing to be fished out of the water.

On weekends, the whole family likes to go walking along the main avenue of Brighton Beach. On a beautiful afternoon many people from the community are outdoors. Russian can be heard everywhere. Shops display all kinds of Russian goods: food, cosmetics, books, even Russian army hats. At nearby Coney Island, Anton and his brother are thrilled with all the super-special rides—the Wonder Wheel, the Go-Karts, and the Cyclone. . . . Well, at least Anton is thrilled. Sasha's not so sure. He begins to feel sick after all the daredevil rides. But he quickly recovers in time to gobble down American hot dogs and delicious ears of corn. Anton sometimes teases his younger brother, but he can also be very protective of him when he is hurt or in trouble.

38

During his stay in this country Anton has already participated in numerous performances. He tries to conserve his own energy for the time when he will be onstage. Hours of rehearsal and days of sitting around are required. He learns a great deal from watching others rehearse. Backstage at a performance of the New York City Ballet production of *Sleeping Beauty,* he listens to dancer Teresa Reyes talk about her role as Carabosse, the wicked fairy. He understands the importance of warming up and being fit and fresh for every performance. This means he must get a lot of rest and exercise and must eat enough of the right foods to give him the energy for long hours of physical activity.

In a performance of *The Nutcracker* at the State University of New York, Anton has his own dressing room, where he makes up for his role as Fritz, the young boy. In this version of *The Nutcracker,* he also performs a lively Russian dance with two other boys. From the wings he watches others dance while sitting next to the nutcracker toy that will soon come alive. There are quiet moments of deep thought as he prepares himself for his time onstage.

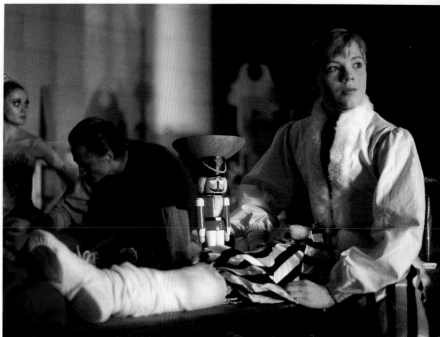

When it is his turn to dance you can sense his mounting exuberance and excitement. Finally he has the opportunity to show what he can do. All the preparation and hard work seem worthwhile. When he receives loud and enthusiastic applause from the audience, he is sure that nothing else could ever feel as good. For Anton, being a dancer is what it's all about!